MATTeR

Rebecca Hunter

www.raintreepublishers.co.uk
Visit our website to find out more information about **Raintree** books.

To order:
☎ Phone 44 (0) 1865 888112
🖹 Send a fax to 44 (0) 1865 314091
🖥 Visit the Raintree Bookshop at www.raintreepublishers.co.uk to browse our catalogue and order online.

First published in Great Britain by Raintree,
Halley Court, Jordan Hill, Oxford
OX2 8EJ, part of Harcourt Education.

Raintree is a registered trademark of Harcourt Education Ltd.

Produced for Raintree by Discovery Books Ltd
Design: Ian Winton
Editorial: Rebecca Hunter
Consultant: Jeremy Bloomfield
Commissioned photography: Chris Fairclough
Illustrations: Keith Williams and Stefan Chabluk
Production: Jonathan Smith

Originated by Dot Gradations Ltd
Printed and bound in China by South China Printing Company

ISBN 1 844 21570 9 (hardback)
07 06 05 04 03
10 9 8 7 6 5 4 3 2 1

ISBN 1 844 21577 6 (paperback)
08 07 06 05 04
10 9 8 7 6 5 4 3 2 1

British Library Cataloguing in Publication Data
Hunter, Rebecca
Matter. – (Discovering Science)
530

A full catalogue record for this book is available from the British Library.

Acknowledgements
The publishers would like to thank the following for permission to reproduce photographs: page **18** bottom (Kim Taylor), Discovery Picture Library: page **6** top; Chris Fairclough: page **4** (all), **12** top, **13** top and right, **14**, **15** ... top, ... **9** top, **24** bottom, **25**, **26** top, **28**, **29** ... on Energy: page **22** top; Oxford Scientific ... page **4** bottom, **18** top (Stan Osolinski); ... Science Photo Library: page **5** (Mehau ... Charles D Winters); gettyimages: page **4** ... **6** bottom (Dan Ham), **9** top (Pal ... bottom (Alan Abramowitz), **12/13** centre (Gavin Hellier), **15** top (Michael Busselle), **17** (David Woodfall), **22** bottom (Peter & Stef Lamberti), **23** (Mark A Leman), **26** bottom (G Brad Lewis), **27** (Michael Rosenfeld), **29** bottom (Larry Ulrich).

Cover photograph of matter in its three states is reproduced with permission of Science Photo Library

The publishers would like to thank the following schools for their help in providing equipment, models and locations for photography sessions: Bedstone College, Bucknell, Moor Park, Ludlow and Packwood Haugh, Shrewsbury.

Every effort has been made to contact copyright holders of any material reproduced in this book.
Any omissions will be rectified in subsequent printings if notice is given to the publishers.

Any words appearing in the text in bold, **like this**, are explained in the Glossary.

CONTENTS

WHAT IS MATTER?

Matter is the name we give to all the stuff in our world. From mountains to marbles, from leopards to ladybirds, everything is made of matter.

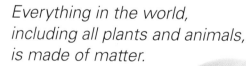

Everything in the world, including all plants and animals, is made of matter.

Many scientists believe that all the matter in the universe was created by an enormous explosion in space called the Big Bang. Some of the energy from this explosion turned into tiny **particles**. These particles make up all the matter that we see today.

STATES OF MATTER

Matter comes in three forms, or states: solids, liquids and gases. Each kind of matter can, under certain conditions, exist as a solid, a liquid and a gas.

The ground you walk on and the walls of your house are solids.

The water in the sea and the things you drink are liquids.

The air that is all around us is made up of gases.

Solids, liquids and gases behave in different ways because of the way they are made up. All types of matter are made of tiny **particles**. They are so tiny we cannot see them. These particles **vibrate**, or move. How much they move depends on how much energy they have. This is what makes solids, liquids and gases so different.

solid

The particles in a solid move around very little. Liquid particles move around more freely. Gas particles have more energy and spread out quickly to fill large spaces.

liquid

gas

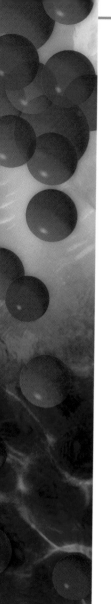

DESCRIBING MATTER

All matter takes up space. This means it has **volume**. Volume is the amount of space that is taken up by matter. It is measured in litres or cubic centimetres or cubic metres.

All matter has **mass**. Mass is the amount of matter in something. You can measure mass on a scale in kilograms and grams.

It is easy to see that not all matter is alike. Some things are heavy, some things are light. Some things stretch, some are brittle. Some things float in water, while other things sink.

◀ Icebergs are huge pieces of floating ice. Eventually they will melt into the sea and disappear. But new icebergs are constantly being formed.

Some things can change their shape, some will not. Some things will pour easily, others do not. Some things feel smooth, while others are rough.

To understand why things behave like this, we need to look at the three different states of matter.

▶ A potter moulds soft clay into a shape that will be useful once it is fired in a kiln to make it hard.

SOLIDS

Some solids are hard and some are soft, but all solids hold their shape unless you do something to change them.

If you break a solid, the pieces will still occupy the same amount of space as before.

This is because the **particles** that make up a solid are held together in a firm structure. These particles do not have enough energy to break out of this structure. Because of this, solids cannot flow in the way liquids and gases do.

There are several types of solids in this picture. They all feel very different to the touch.

PROJECT

Solids have many properties that we find useful. Try this experiment to look at a few of them.

You will need:

a bowl of water

a magnet

a collection of solid objects, such as a pencil, a coin, a key, a wooden spoon, a paper clip, a rock, a plastic ruler, a piece of aluminium foil, a rubber, a cork.

You are going to do three tests on these solids.

Test 1. Does the solid bend? (Try gently to bend it, but do not break it!)

Test 2. Does the solid float? (Put it in the bowl of water.)

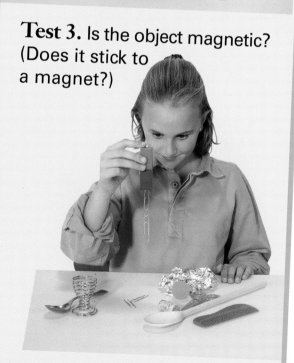

Test 3. Is the object magnetic? (Does it stick to a magnet?)

You can record your results in a chart. Do you notice anything about certain groups of solids?

USES OF SOLIDS

The different **properties** of solids mean we can use them in many ways.

The **transparency** and strength of glass is what makes it a perfect material for packaging foods and drinks in jars and bottles. Glass is also useful for windows. It lets light in and lets us see out.

Diamonds are the hardest solids we know. Nothing can cut a diamond except another diamond.

The strength of iron and steel means they are very useful for making machines and for making strong buildings.

Aluminium is a very light metal and is useful in making aeroplanes.

Plastics have become very important to us because of their light weight, strength, and flexibility.

Polystyrene is a plastic that is very **buoyant**. This means that it floats. Because of this it is often used in life jackets.

▼ *There are many strong materials being used on this building site.*

LIQUIDS

When a substance is a liquid, its **particles** have more energy than the particles in a solid. This means the liquid can move easily, or flow. Liquids have no definite shape. They have a fixed **volume**, but their shape depends on the shape of their container.

HOW LIQUIDS FLOW

Liquids can be thick or thin. They can pour easily or with difficulty. Because liquids flow, they are called **fluids**.

▲ Water has a low viscosity and flows very easily.

Viscosity measures how easily a liquid flows. If a liquid flows slowly, its viscosity is high. If it flows quickly, its viscosity is low.

Honey has a high viscosity and flows slowly.

DENSITY OF LIQUIDS

A liquid's **properties** depend on its **viscosity** and also its **density**. Density compares the **mass**, or the amount of matter in something, to its **volume**. Liquids with a low density will float on top of liquids with a higher density.

The cream on this cup of coffee is less dense than the coffee, and so it floats on top.

PROJECT

This experiment compares the densities of three different liquids.

2. Leave them to settle and see what happens.

You will need:
an equal measure of vegetable oil, water and syrup
a tall glass.

1. Mix the three liquids together in the glass.

Liquids that are less dense than water will float above it.

Liquids that are denser than water, will sink below it.

Which liquid here has the lowest density? Which has the highest?

Oil is less dense than water and, therefore, floats on top of it. When oil tankers run aground at sea, oil escapes into the water and forms a slick, or film of oil, on the surface. An oil slick is very harmful to wildlife. Animals and birds that live and feed at sea are often trapped in the oil. The oil clogs their feathers or fur. This makes it impossible for them to swim, keep warm or find food. They usually die of cold and hunger.

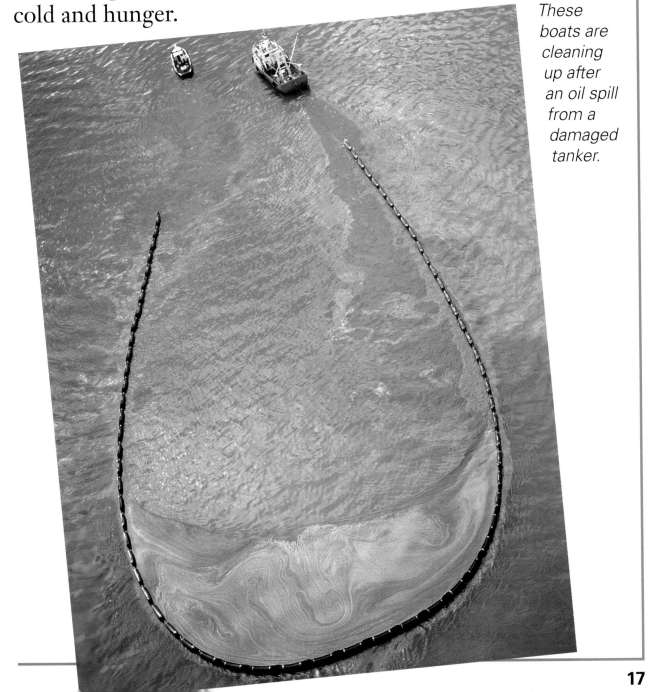

These boats are cleaning up after an oil spill from a damaged tanker.

SURFACE TENSION

The **particles** in a liquid pull towards each other equally in all directions. This is what makes liquids form drops when they fall on a surface. Each drop looks as if it is held in place by a skin. This effect is called **surface tension**.

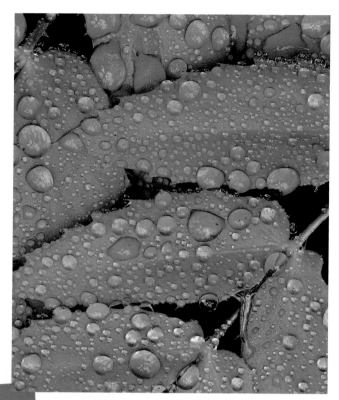

▲ *Water droplets form on plant leaves after a shower of rain.*

A pond skater can walk on the surface of water because of surface tension.

Surface tension can easily be seen in water in the way pond insects appear to walk on water. The surface tension holds their weight, and their feet just make little dents in the surface of the water. **Polluting** water destroys its surface tension. Surface-living insects cannot live in polluted ponds and rivers.

Bubbles are also examples of surface tension. Surface tension pulls bubbles into the shape of a sphere, or a ball.

PROJECT

See how surface tension is broken by polluting water with a detergent such as washing-up liquid.

You will need:
a shallow dish
some water
a few matches
some washing-up liquid.

1. Fill the dish with water and let it settle.

3. Add a drop of washing-up liquid to the centre of the dish. Watch what happens.

The washing-up liquid breaks the surface tension in the centre of the dish.

The matches move to the edge of the dish where the surface tension is stronger.

2. Carefully float a few matches on the surface in a pattern.

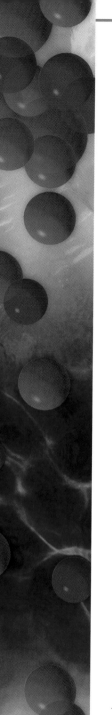

WATER

Water is easily the most important liquid in our world. Oceans cover over two-thirds of Earth's surface. Even more water is stored on land in rivers and lakes.

All living things are made mostly of water. Our own bodies are about 60 per cent water by weight.

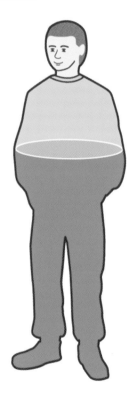

A tomato is almost totally made of water, (95 per cent water).

People use huge amounts of water every day. We need to drink about 2 litres of water a day to stay healthy. (This is equal to eight glasses a day.) We use much more than that in cooking and washing.

PROJECT

Be a water-use watcher!

Work out how much water your family uses in one day.

1. How much do you use in cooking? Measure how much water is used to prepare each meal.

2. Get your family to time how long they spend in the shower. Then turn the shower on and measure in a bucket how much water comes out in a minute.

3. Find out how much water the toilet uses by filling the tank by bucket. Make your family keep a chart of how many times they flush it in a day.

4. Find out how much water the washing machine and dishwasher use. (The manual that comes with the machine may tell you this.)

Don't forget to include: all the water you drink in squash, coffee, tea and cocoa; cleaning your teeth; watering the garden; cleaning the car.

What is your total? Is it more than you expected? You could draw a chart to record your results.

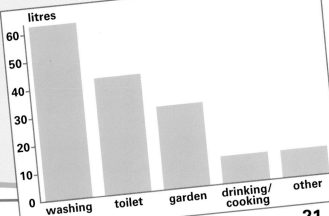

WATER IN INDUSTRY

Water has many uses in industry. Power stations use huge amounts of water to create steam to drive **generators**. Other industries use water to cool furnaces, or to clean materials and equipment.

▶ *Steam rises from cooling towers at a power station.*

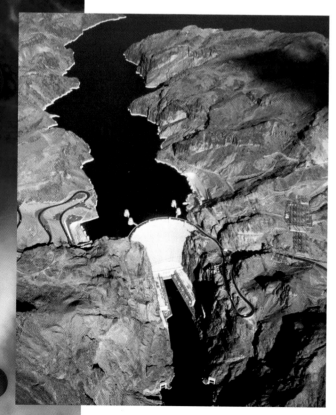

WATER AND ENERGY

Water is also an important provider of energy. About 20 per cent of the world's energy comes from hydroelectric power (HEP). In an HEP station, the energy of falling water drives **turbines** that then drive an electric generator.

The Hoover Dam holds back Lake Mead, the largest artificial lake in the USA and provides HEP for much of California, Nevada and Arizona.

OTHER LIQUIDS

Other liquids are also important to us. Crude oil can be made into many useful products: petrol for car fuel, kerosene for heating and lighting, gas oil for central heating fuel and many types of plastics.

This oil rig is drilling for oil under the seabed.

GASES

Unlike solids and liquids, gases have no fixed **volume** and no fixed shape. Gases have these **properties** because their **particles** have so much energy that they move completely freely. Some gases like bromine or iodine vapour are coloured and can be seen easily, but most gases are invisible and difficult to identify.

▶ *Iodine is a purple solid that turns into a purple gas very easily.*

We can feel the gases in the atmosphere. If you are outside on a windy day, or standing by an open window, you can feel the air blow on you. Over 75 per cent of the air is made up of the gas nitrogen. Nearly 25 per cent is made up of the gas oxygen. Oxygen is the most important gas in the atmosphere. Without it plants and animals could not live on the planet.

It would be difficult to fly a kite without the wind!

WEIGHING GASES

Since you cannot see most gases, you might think they weigh nothing. This is not true. All gases are made of particles and, therefore, have **mass**.

PROJECT

Show that gases have mass.

You will need:
two identical balloons
a wooden stick
some string.

1. Blow up both balloons and tie one to each end of the stick.

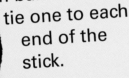

2. Suspend the stick so that the balloons are balanced.

3. Burst one of the balloons. What happens?

The remaining balloon still contains gas particles, so it is heavier than the burst balloon.

These balloons are filled with a gas called helium. Helium is a lighter gas than air, so a balloon filled with helium will float away.

CHANGING STATES

Substances can exist in more than one physical state. They change from one state to another because of the way their **particles** behave. This usually happens with a change in temperature.

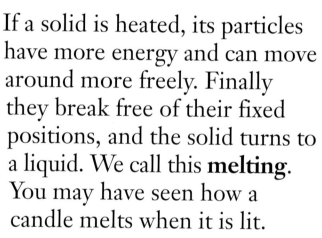

▶ *Once it is lighted, a solid candle melts and turns into liquid wax.*

If a solid is heated, its particles have more energy and can move around more freely. Finally they break free of their fixed positions, and the solid turns to a liquid. We call this **melting**. You may have seen how a candle melts when it is lit.

When a liquid is cooled, its particles slow down, and finally the substance becomes a solid.

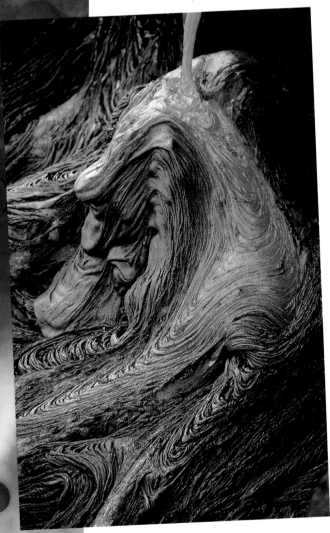

Rock deep inside Earth is at such a high temperature that it is liquid. When this molten rock comes to the surface, it cools down and becomes a solid.

The way that solids and liquids change states can be very useful to us. Both metals and glass become liquids when they are heated to high temperatures. Once they are **molten**, they can be moulded into useful shapes. When they are cooled they become hard, and we can use them for many purposes.

Iron is made into steel in a furnace. The molten steel is then poured into a mould to cool and solidify.

EVAPORATION

When a liquid is heated, its **particles** move around faster and faster. Finally they **evaporate** into a gas.

PROJECT

See how water evaporates.

You will need:
a jug of water
an area of concrete or paving
some chalk
a sunny day!

1. Pour the water on to the ground to make a large puddle.

2. Draw around the edge of the puddle with the chalk.

3. Come back in an hour and mark the outline of the puddle with chalk again.

4. Repeat this every hour until the puddle has disappeared.

The water has not really gone, it has evaporated and become a gas.

These wet clothes will dry as the water evaporates from them.

CONDENSATION

When gases are cooled, the opposite happens. The particles slow down and turn back into liquids. This is called **condensation**. You can see this happening on cold days in winter. Water vapour condenses into water droplets on windows.

▲ *Water vapour condenses into droplets on windows on cold days.*

Water is a most unusual type of matter because it is found naturally on Earth in all three states. Can you identify them all in this picture?

GLOSSARY

buoyant something that floats well

condensation process by which a gas changes into a liquid

density mass per unit volume of a substance

evaporation change of a substance from a liquid into a gas

fluid flowing substance that is either a liquid or a gas

generator machine that turns heat or movement energy into electrical energy

mass amount of matter in an object

melting change of a substance from solid to liquid

molten when a substance melts and becomes liquid

particles tiny parts of a substance

pollution substances that dirty or harm the environment

properties features or qualities, particular to an object or thing. Strength and flexibility are examples of properties.

surface tension effect that makes a liquid appear to have a 'skin'

transparency how easily you can see through something

turbine machine that is made to rotate to drive a generator

vibration quick back-and-forth movement

viscosity measure of how easily a liquid flows

volume space occupied by matter

FURTHER INFORMATION

BOOKS

Chemicals in Action: States of Matter, Chris Oxlade
(Heinemann Library, 2002)
Explore Science: Materials and their properties, Angela Royston
(Heinemann Library, 2003)
Materials all Around us: Solids, Liquids and Gases,
Robert Snedden (Heinemann Library, 2001)
Matter, Christopher Cooper (Dorling Kindersley
Publishing, 2000)

WEBSITES

Creative Chemistry – a fun, interactive site with puzzles, games, information
and links to other interesting websites.
http://www.creative-chemistry.org.uk

BrainPOP – Matter and Molecules – experiments to learn about the
building blocks of the universe including mass and density, atoms, the pH scale
and water.
http://www.brainpop.com/science/matter/

Explore Science – access a library of information on many science topics.
Includes photos and artwork, video and animation, activities and tests.
http://www.heinemannexplore.com

INDEX

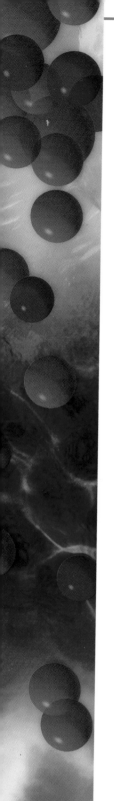